Cow Candy

A Dance of Art and Poetry

Nolcha Fox and Vangie Hansen

Cyberwit.net
HIG 45 Kaushambi Kunj, Kalindipuram
Allahabad - 211011 (U.P.) India
http://www.cyberwit.net
Tel: +(91) 9415091004
E-mail: info@cyberwit.net

Printed at Quarterfold Printabilities.

Author Acknowledgements

Thanks to *Wilder Literature* for publishing "Love Is a Fish." Thanks to *Duck Head Journal* for publishing "Best Revenge" and "Unnecessary" (under the title "Self-Portrait"). Thanks to Medusa's Kitchen for publishing all the poems in this book, except "Someone Is Leaving." Thanks to *Poetica Review* for publishing "Someone Is Leaving."

Thanks to Sarah, Tony, Lyndi, and Tom for reading first drafts and cheering me on.

Thanks to my family, who made me what I am.

Artist Acknowledgements

Thanks to poet Nolcha Fox for suggesting a collaboration between a poet and an artist. Multi-media presentation enhances appreciation and enjoyment to everyone who opens this book. Win-win!

Sincere appreciation to my parents for their unwavering support of my artistic endeavors throughout many decades. Thanks to my daughter, Beth Marshall, for always being vocal in her praise and wonder at my art. Having people who believe in me helps to boost me to a higher plane...thank you dear ones.

Contents

Love is a Fish 7

Blame the Racoon 9

Best Revenge 11

Colors Are Running 13

Cow Candy 15

Unnecessary 17

Rumor 19

Old Barn 21

Coming West 23

Someone Is Leaving 25

Woman Awash 27

Rusty 29

Serenade 31

When a Tree Falls 33

Love is a Fish

With Apologies to Lyndi

Love is not a bird
bursting out of my body
at the sound of a voice,
the touch of a hand.

No, love is a fish,
flopping on dry land,
gasping for air,
killing flies with its stink.

And I'm a fisherman,
good only for telling tails,
about the ones that got away
(they were THIS big).

So how did I catch you?

Blame the Racoon

I throw open my front door,
to find things are missing. Again.
The potted tomato plant,
missing tomatoes.
The umbrella I set out
to dry on the porch,
twirled to oblivion.
And where's my yellow
Volkswagen Beetle?
Did it elope with
a butterfly?
Blame Robber Racoon,
the neighborhood scourge,
says Miss Lee next door.
I think I know the real thief.
It's sunrise, creeping
on tiptoe, trampling
the roses, stealing the night.
Eating the tomatoes,
taking my car for a
joy ride (I'll find it later,
halfway down the street).
Stomping mud on the
sidewalk, spinning my
umbrella, before getting
down to the business of the day.

But if I find my umbrella
up in the tree, it's definitely
Robber Racoon.

Best Revenge

Who is that woman
in the mirror?
It must be my mother,
not me.

I am a much
younger version
of the woman
that I see.

I wrap myself in
robes of joy,
more tightly
in my boundaries.

With a spade
I dig a hole
and plant
my feet.

The best revenge
is to blossom.

Colors Are Running

Colors are running, rain on a painting.
They streak nude through the streets.
Rose, turquoise, purple, they reach up to moonlight,
they dance on the roof to the beat of the rain.
Purple stops at Mom's place to go through old photos.
Turquoise grabs a latte, then leaps into bed.
Rose steals my car, then blows through a stop sign.
I get the ticket, and win a cigar.

11/04/2011

Cow Candy

When the nurses
were nodding,
a cow unpeeled
itself from
the nursery wall.
"That one,"
she mooed.
A good mama,
she licked my
head, a lollipop.
Now my hair
whorls and swirls
every which way,
a blender
disaster.
Invectives
don't impress it.
Hair clips
and curlers,
brief relief.
Five minutes
later, my mane
is insane.

The final
solution,
cut it down
to the nub.

Unnecessary

I know I'm in your way,
a coat rack that you
blame for bruises,
a lampshade that you
bump at night.

I know that you don't
find me useful,
I know and yet I wait.
I wait and spill cream
on your sweater,
If you won't love me,
I'll take hate.

I wait for you to take my key,
and shove me out the door.
Instead, you treat me
like a portrait
hanging on the wall.
Something barely
noticed, something
you acquired.

Rumor

Someone spread
an elaborate
rumor about me.
Something about
growing wings,
sliding down
rainbows,
rappelling
through clouds.
Someone thinks
my feet have
detached from
the ground,
that I can't
be trusted
to be normal,
humdrum,
stodgy.

Rumor?
I think
It's truth.

Old Barn

You make me brake,
you take my breath,
I park my car and ponder,
every time I drive this road.

What would I find if I walked in?
Perhaps some mice,
some cats and sheep
take shelter in your belly.

Perhaps you house
a child's laugh, some
rusted tools, the
haunting ghosts of famine.

Perhaps I'd find the love I left
for one I thought was better.
But you will never let me go,
you always bring me home.

Cow Candy

Coming West

We began our journey west
when I was still a baby.
Hurricane Diane with wind and rain
pushed our car ahead of her.
My parents in a hurry,
they didn't want to shelter.
Perhaps they thought
they'd change their minds,
or the service call my father back.
It might have been the only time
my parents were not late.

Someone Is Leaving

Hunger for new is the opposite of a lilac tree.
Bags and suitcases are a kiss goodbye.
The mother sobs, a rainbow of fear.
Shadows enclose her glistening raincoat.
The windows behind her are shut to revelation.
The sweep of her hair is a trail of birdseed.
Someone is leaving. Adieu.

Woman Awash

I can be flooded,
tossed by waves,
while standing on dry land.

One sunny day
floods me with warmth, and
tosses the shoes off my feet.

Rusty

You say that I'm just rusty,
too old to care, neglected,
my clothes all worn and faded.
You say I'm out of practice,
my mind decayed, too sleepy.

Just don't forget that rust is used
to polish gold and silver.
It takes away your itching.
I'll take it as a compliment,
Rust is not too shabby.

Serenade

I'll serenade you long and sweet,
a low romance, some swaying hips,
I'll be your reed, your vibrant pulse
until the cows come home.
And that's a long, long time.

When a Tree Falls

When a tree falls,
and I don't hear it,
does it make a sound?

When a rainbow paints the sky,
and I don't see it,
was there any rain?

When you want me
and I don't know it,
are there any tears?

When I close my eyes
for one last time,
will the world exist?